101 USES FOR A JOHN MAJOR

101 USES FOR A JOHN MAJOR

PATRICK WRIGHT & PETER RICHARDSON

ANDRE DEUTSCH

First published
in Great Britain in 1993 by
André Deutsch Limited
106 Great Russell Street
London WC1B 3LJ

Cataloguing-in-Publication data available for
this title from the British Library

ISBN 0 233 98862 9

Printed in Great Britain by
WBC, Bridgend

Dedicated
not altogether unrespectfully
to John Major. Oh yes.

Acknowledgements

Special thanks to Peter R., Peter V., Graham and all at the Red Lion, Fernhurst. Richard C., Esther, Tom, Tony R. and all at Private Eye. Richard and all at Smugglers Wines.

Foreword

'John Major's useless,' said Graham, as he slipped from his stool to the floor of the Red Lion.

I glanced at Peter. It was clear he was not inconsiderably irritated by Graham's condemnation of the man whose decisive leadership delivered us from the ERM: the man who enthralled our nation with the Maastricht debate: the man who enraptured us with his vision of a nation full of motorway lavatories and free of motorway cones, oh yes. A man whose very underpants have enchanted us for nearly three years. It was, in my judgement, time that Peter and I left the Red Lion.

Outside, on the village green, the evening air carried the sound of old ladies cycling around in the church and drinking warm beer. Several bastards, out for a stroll, cast lengthening shadows. Peter was silent.

'In my judgement, you are not inconsiderably silent, Peter,' I said.

'It's John,' said Peter, picking something from his nose. 'I'm in no small measure irritated by the way Graham keeps on and on about John Major being useless. It is my judgement that our Prime Minister is extremely useful, and not inconsiderably so. Oh, yes.'

'Oh, yes,' I concurred.

'Would it not be a notion of no small merit if we were to compile a compilation of Mr. Major's innumerable attributes?'

'Oh, yes,' I said, after not a few moments of time had passed.

'You see, Patrick, if we allow people like Graham to put it about that our leader is useless then others may come to be of the same opinion. And that, in my judgement, would be in no small measure deleterious to the prospects of the Conservative party.'

'Oh, yes,' I said, alarmed by this possibility.

And so it was, on that balmy evening in June, that we resolved to counter Graham's calumny and to bring to public notice the many uses for a John Major.

PATRICK WRIGHT was born in 1945 in North Wales. Apart from publishing seven books of his own cartoons, he has worked extensively in advertising and all forms of publishing. He lives in West Sussex, along with his long-suffering wife and children. His sole interest is John Major.

PETER RICHARDSON was born in 1951 in Warwickshire. A graphic artist, he has worked extensively in animation, advertising and publishing. He lives in East Sussex with his wife and two children and his main interest, between listening to the radio at hourly intervals, is Formula One Grand Prix.

AN ELEGANT AND NOT INCONSIDERABLY UNBEAUTIFUL MONUMENT TO THE CONSERVATIVE PARTY'S ACHIEVEMENTS IN NEWBURY, CHRISTCHURCH, ETC, ETC.

A COMPANION FOR EX-PRIME MINISTERS.
(OR, ONE OF THEM, AT LEAST.)

A PANTOMIME MOLLUSC
(WITH A DODGY AGENT)

A FRIEND FOR NORMAN LAMONT

A SLEEPING POLICEMAN

PRUNING SHEARS.

A SELF-PROPELLED WHEEL BARROW.

AN ATTRACTIVE GARDEN GNOME.

A SUPPORT FOR YOUR SAPLING.

A NOT INCONSIDERABLY IRRITATING WHEELCLAMP

SOMETHING YOU CAN SAFELY LEAVE BY THE ROADSIDE.

MASCOT FOR A DUSTCART.

AN ORGAN GRINDER'S MONKEY.

A PET FOR SOMEONE WHO HATES PETS

A NOT INCONSIDERABLY IMPRESSIVE PLANT POT STAND

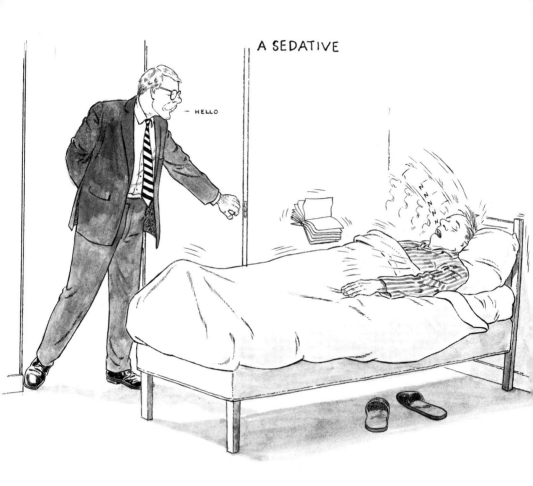

A NOT UNUNIQUE TEAS-MADE

A HOOVER

AN IRONING BOARD

SOMETHING TO STIR YOUR PAINT WITH

LAGGING FOR YOUR PIPES.

A DECOY TURKEY

GUARD FOR YOUR LETTUCE

A REALLY SATISFYING SCRATCHING POST FOR CATS

DOG FOOD ?

TARGET CHANGER AT A GUN CLUB

A SANDBAG.

A USEFUL DEVICE FOR OPENING LOCKED DOORS.

A LETTER BOX

A TURN STILE.

A PERIPATETIC PARK BENCH

A BAR STOOL

A NOT INCONSIDERABLY PROVOCATIVE CYCLE STAND

BALLAST FOR A HOT AIR BALLOON

A NOT INCONSIDERABLY USEFUL DIGIT FOR STARTING MODEL AERO ENGINES

AN ANCHOR.

A COMPANION FOR YOUR FISH.

A VERSATILE BOOKEND.

A NOT ENTIRELY PLEASING TOAST RACK

A TOWN-CRYER

A TRAIN SPOTTER'S ANORAK

A JUMBLE SALE 'SMURF'

THE BEGINNING OF A QUEUE

A BUS STOP.

A CLOWN.

SOAP

AN EXECUTIVE TOY

SECURITY GUARD.

A HOSTAGE

A PIT PROP

A DIGGER OF MANY NOT INCONSIDERABLE HOLES.

JOHN MAJOR — NEWS AT TEN
HASLEMERE ...

FEARLESS WAR CORRESPONDENT
IN WAR TORN HASLEMERE.

A NOT INCONSIDERABLY UNAPPEALING REGIMENTAL MASCOT

A NOT INCONSIDERABLY OFFENSIVE AND INFURIATING GARGOYLE.

A WEATHER VANE

A DRAUGHT EXCLUDER.

AN INGENIOUS APPARATUS FOR MOISTENING THE
REVERSE SIDE OF STAMPS PRIOR TO AFFIXING THEM
TO THE FACE OF ENVELOPES . OH, YES.

A LAVATORY PAPER HOLDER.

UNSIGHTLY HAIR REMOVER.
(A DEVICE FOR REMOVING UNSIGHTLY HAIR, THAT IS. THE DEVICE ITSELF IS NOT UNSIGHTLY, OH NO.)

A CASTAWAY.

A DECK CHAIR ATTENDANT AT THE NORTH POLE.

A HOLE IN THE WALL CASH DISPENSER

A NOT UNUSEFUL PAPER SHREDDER

A DUMB WAITER.

"A SAFE PAIR OF HANDS"

A CABER FOR THE HIGHLAND GAMES

A SUBSTITUTE CHIPPENDALE

SAUCY CENTRE-FOLD IN 'FARMERS WEEKLY'

A CLAPPER IN A BELL.

DUNG

PATRICK WRIGHT 93

A STEPPING STONE

A RUSTIC PLOUGH

A FENCE POST

THIS IS YOUR AMAZING FREE GIFT! YOUR VERY OWN, FULL COLOUR, TWO DIMENSIONAL REPLICA OF A JOHN MAJOR! ALL YOU NEED TO COMPLETE THIS FANTASTIC KIT IS A PAIR OF SCISSORS, A PIECE OF CARD, SOME PAPER GLUE AND A LITTLE STRING. FOLLOW THESE SIMPLE INSTRUCTIONS : 1. CUT ROUND THE OUTLINES OF BOTH FRONT AND BACK FIGURES. 2. TRACE ROUND ONE FIGURE ON TO THE CARD. 3. CUT OUT CARD FIGURE. 4. GLUE FRONT AND BACK FIGURES TO THE CARD. 5. PIERCE THE HOLE ON TOP OF THE HEAD AND THREAD STRING THROUGH IT. YOU CAN HANG YOUR REPLICA JOHN MAJOR FROM YOUR CAR MIRROR, OR NEAR AN OPEN WINDOW. HOURS OF FUN GUARANTEED!

FRONT

BACK

AN AMAZING FREE GIFT.

A Note From The Authors

It won't have escaped the reader's notice that, in spite of its title, there are in fact only seventy-four possible uses for a John Major in this little book. This is because another book is planned for next year. Oh, yes. But this time the authors would like you, the not inconsiderably great British public, to participate.

So, if you can dream up further uses for our Prime Minister, why not fill in the coupon at the end of this book and send it to the Post Office Box Number provided. Blank pages are also provided for those who would like to have a go at drawing our John. Don't forget to print your name on the coupon so you can be credited with your idea. Of course, all this rather depends on our Mr. Major hanging on to his job.

IF YOU HAVE ENJOYED THIS LITTLE BOOK
AND WOULD LIKE TO CONTRIBUTE YOUR
OWN IDEAS TOWARDS 'A FURTHER 101 USES
FOR A JOHN MAJOR', PLEASE JOT THEM DOWN
ON THE SPACES BELOW AND SEND THEM TO :
WRIGHT. P.O.BOX 78 . HASLEMERE.SURREY.
                                    GU 27 3 XZ

I THINK JOHN MAJOR MIGHT BE USEFUL AS A ...

1.

2.

3.

4.

5.

NAME & ADDRESS (ADDRESS ONLY IF YOU WANT A REPLY)

I WISH TO BE CREDITED WITH MY IDEA IN 'A FURTHER
101 USES FOR A JOHN MAJOR'. YES . NO.
TWO BLANK PAGES ARE PROVIDED FOR THOSE
WHO MIGHT WISH TO SUBMIT DRAWINGS .